Southwood Books Limited
3–5 Islington High Street
London N1 9LQ

First published in Australia by Roland Harvey Books, 1997

This edition published in the UK under licence from
Penguin Books Australia Ltd by Southwood Books Limited, 2002

ISBN 1 903207 81 9

Copyright © Rolf Heimann, 1997

Designed by Romany Glover

A CIP catalogue record for this book is available from the British Library

Printed in China by Everbest Printing Co. Ltd

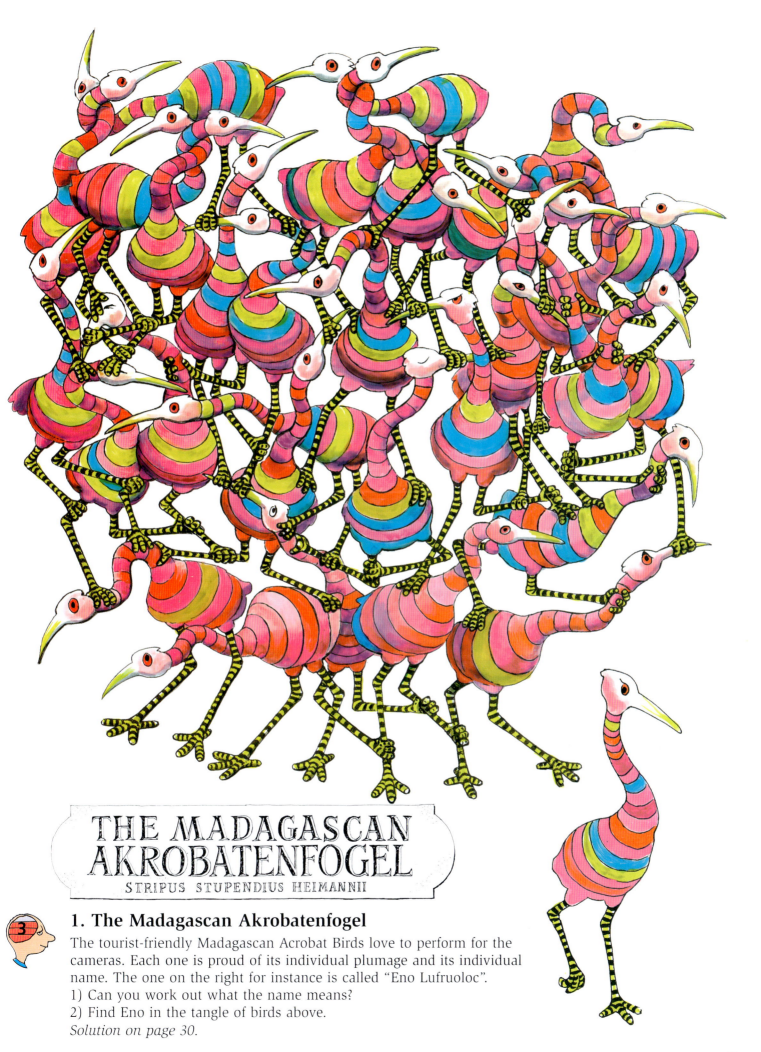

THE MADAGASCAN AKROBATENFOGEL
STRIPUS STUPENDIUS HEIMANNII

1. The Madagascan Akrobatenfogel

The tourist-friendly Madagascan Acrobat Birds love to perform for the cameras. Each one is proud of its individual plumage and its individual name. The one on the right for instance is called "Eno Lufruoloc".

1) Can you work out what the name means?

2) Find Eno in the tangle of birds above.

Solution on page 30.

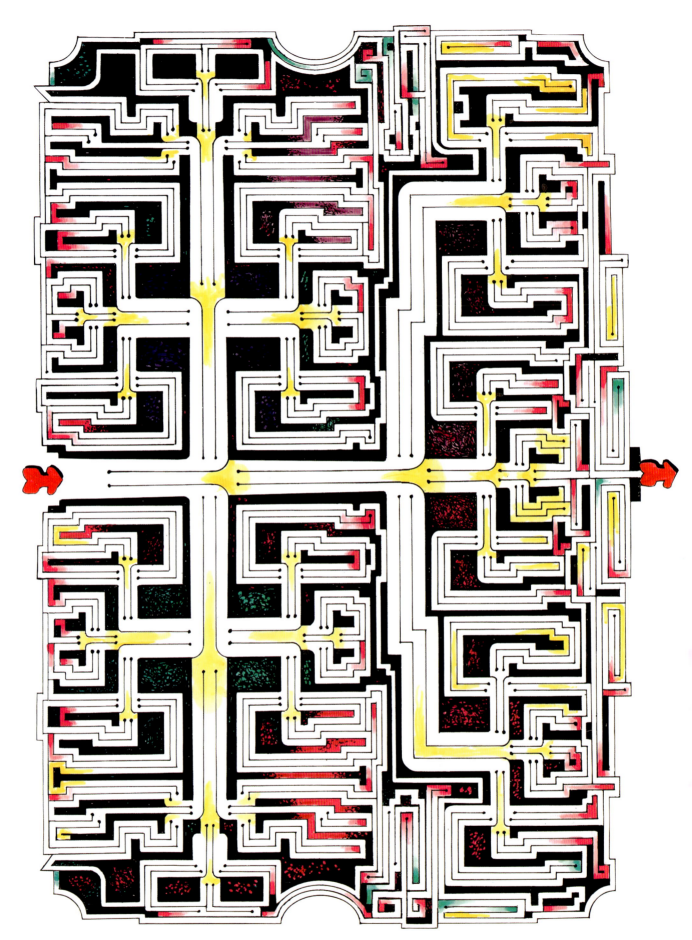

2. Hindsight

Imagine, as you walk down the street, your path splits into three every hour. Within five hours, that leaves you the choice of no less than 243 different possibilities! Of course, if you trace the path from the point of exit, it seems so much simpler! When going through life, this is called hindsight. When going through a maze, it is called cheating. See how you go with this one.

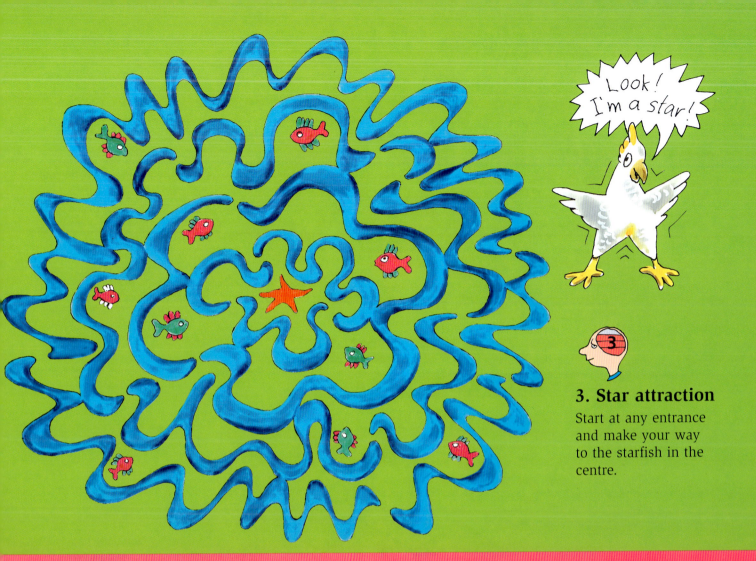

Look! I'm a star!

3. Star attraction

Start at any entrance and make your way to the starfish in the centre.

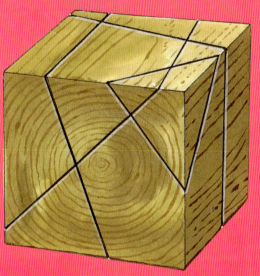

4. Cube cut

If this cube is cut as pictured, how many pieces will you get?
Solution on page 30.

5. Spherical numerical

If the sphere is cut five times as pictured, how many pieces will you get?
Solution on page 30.

A   B   C   D

6. Back to front

One of these line drawings shows the same cube from the reverse side. Three of the drawings are incorrect. Find the right one!
Solution on page 30.

12. Dazzling dice

How many dots should be on the blank side of the die? *Solution on page 30.*

13. Around the blocks

As you can see, the cubes have been strung on a rope like pearls on a string.
If Conny pulls the five ropes tight, the blocks will form a picture.
Solution on page 30.

14. Crown camouflage

Only one of these Royal crowns is the genuine one, as represented in the picture above.
Solution on page 30.

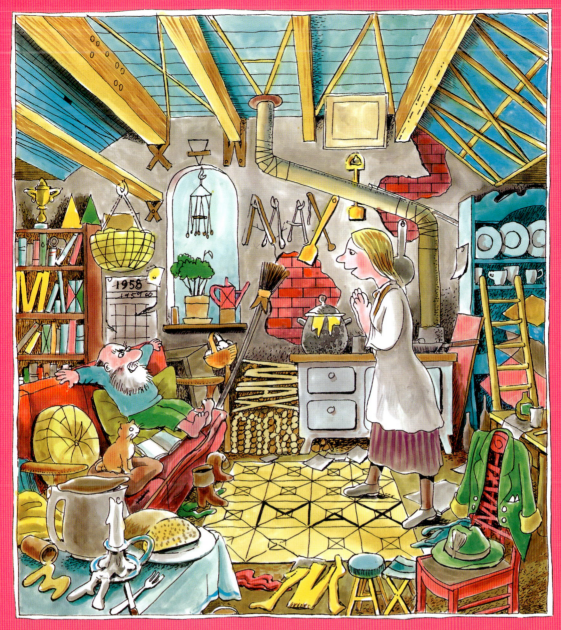

15. Who is that man?

Mr Rumpelstiltskin was a very difficult employer. Before he would give any applicant the job of housekeeper, he asked them to guess his first name.

"Come on now," he said, "it's not so hard. My first name appears no less than 22 times in this room!" *Solution on page 30.*

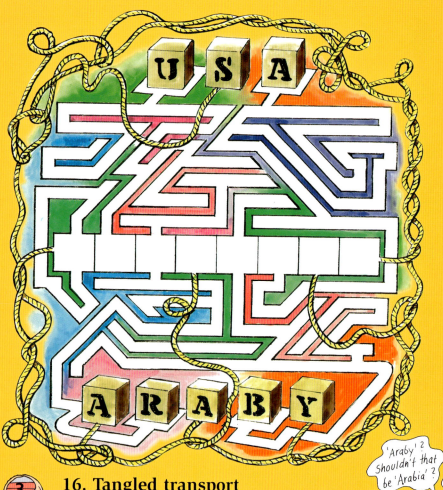

16. Tangled transport

We can see where the eight boxes come from. But where will they be shipped to? Find out by unravelling the rope and solving the maze.
Solution on page 30.

'Araby'? Shouldn't that be 'Arabia'?

Not if the boxes contain frankincense and myrrh!

17. Long labels

The six items of cargo all have different destinations and they have been secretly marked with the names of these port cities. Can you read them?
Solution on page 30.

18. Tall tales

We know that we can read elongated letters if we look at them at a sharp angle from below. But can you still read the letters if they have been elongated a lot?
Solution on page 30.

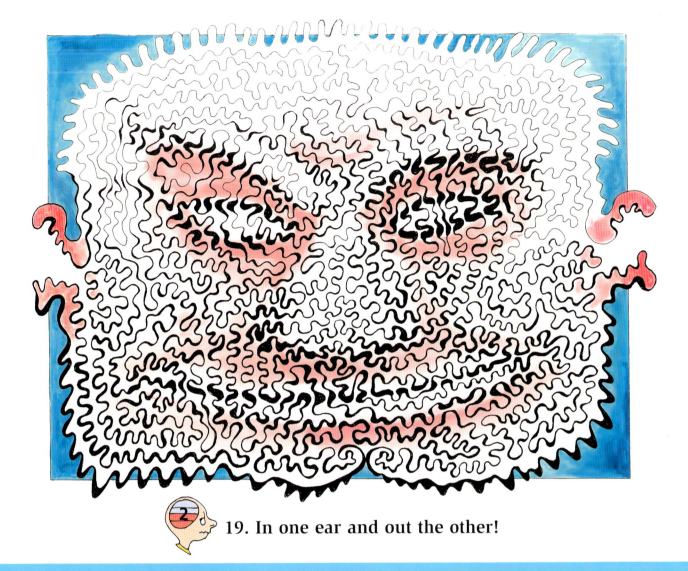

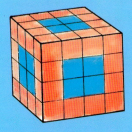 19. In one ear and out the other!

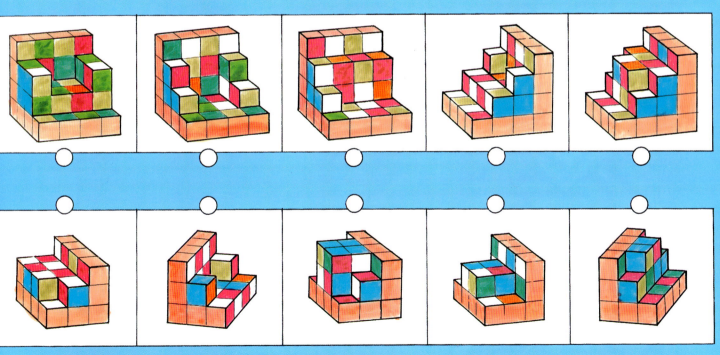

 ## 20. Cube conundrum

Each shape in the lower row fits perfectly into one of the shapes in the upper row to make up a cube, as pictured. But which shape fits where? *Solution on page 30.*

21. Time lapse

Detective McQuick was not as easily fooled as one of his colleagues who said, "The sign gives us a good indication which of the two pictures was taken first".

The Escher
BELVÉDÈRE
Restoration
Appeal

$6000
$5000
$4000
$3000
$2000
$1000

DANGER
KEEP
OUT

PARK

"Look again," said Detective McQuick. "Someone is deliberately trying to fool us with this sign. And they even cut back some of the bushes! Nevertheless I'm pretty sure the picture on the left was taken first." There are six items in the picture which would appear to confirm McQuick's theory. *Solution on page 30.*

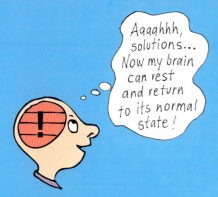

Aaaghhh, solutions... Now my brain can rest and return to its normal state !

Solutions

1. **The Madagascan Akrobatenfogel** (page 3) Read "Eno Lufruoloc" backwards!

4. **Cube cut** (page 5) Cube divides into 9 pieces.

5. **Spherical numerical** (page 5) Sphere divides into 18 pieces.

6. **Back to front** (page 5) Drawing D shows the cube from the back.

7. **Find the pair** (page 6) If the hexagons are correctly connected and the lines cross out the right letters, the remaining letters spell: Berlin Paris Lima Ottawa Madrid Brasilia Apia London.

8. **Weight watch** (page 6) The missing total is 55kg. Each chest weighs 20kg, each suitcase weighs 15kg, each bag weighs 5kg, each barrel weighs 10kg.

10. **Don't blow your stack!** (page 7)

11. **Good timing** (pages 8 & 9) The house they're looking for is just to the left of the church with the two towers. The clock on the left tower is more likely to be right because its time is also shown on three other clocks.

12. **Dazzling dice** (page 10) Each pair of dice has together a total of 6 dots, so the blank one should show one dot.

13. **Around the blocks** (page 10)

14. **Crown camouflage** (page 10) The second crown from the left is the correct one.

15. **Who is that man?** (page 11)
"Max" in Morse Code – – · – · · –   "Max" in Braille

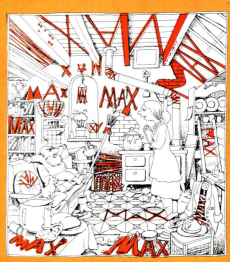

16. **Tangled transport** (page 12) "Surabaya"

17. **Long labels** (page 12) The goods come from Rio de Janeiro, Hamburg, Gdansk, Singapore, Marseilles and Bombay.

18. **Tall tales** (page 12) If viewed from an angle, the letters spell out: YES YOU CAN DO IT

20. **Cube conundrum** (page 13)

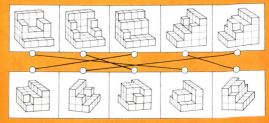

21. **Time lapse** (pages 14 & 15) The building on the left is still being built in the first picture, and the parking sign is still being painted. In the right picture the orchard behind the parking sign has bigger trees, the railing on top has deteriorated, more plaster has fallen off in four different places, the plant on top has grown, and the tip has fallen off the right tower.

22. **From hex to hex** (page 16) The third path from the right will get you through.

23. **Draw a blank** (page 16) The first row of pictures is arranged in the colour spectrum of the rainbow. The purple/violet is missing, hence the boat picture will fit in.

. **Shaping a city** (page 17) The city names which fill the blank spaces are: Sydney, Athens, Moscow, Pisa, New York, London, Berlin, Paris.

. **Make the connection** (page 18) Bird is to fish as plane is to boat. Paw is to cat as tyre is to car. Mouth is to face as door is to house. Cheese is to mouse as worm is to hen. "Leaf is to tree..." has no partner.

. **Mass of cubes** (page 18) "CUBES" is the word.

. **Egyptian cat-a-combs** (page 19)

. **Pagoda** (page 19) The second floor from the top and the second floor from the bottom have a round pattern within the railing.

. **Upstairs, downstairs** (page 19) The upright and the flat sections of the stairs are opposite at left and right.

. **Scare the crow** (pages 20 & 21)

. **Colourful antics** (page 22) Seven red ants and seven green ants can escape.

. **Pussy's place** (page 22) Looking at the three cat panels, both horizontally and vertically, you'll get a total of one black cat (total of one black head, one black body, one black tail), so the missing panel must be filled by a white cat with a black tail.

33. **Can you imagine?** (page 23) This is the sight from Conny's point of view.

34. **Scrambled squares** (page 23) 'A' and 'B' are wrong. The letters, when unscrambled, spell 'NEST'.

35. **Dualism** (page 24) Put the painting upright and hold a mirror to each half!

36. **Shaping up** (page 24)

37. **Mix 'n' match** (page 25) Block 'E' fits into Block 'A'. Block 'A' has two more small cubes than Block 'E'.

38. **All tied up** (page 26) The cat is anchored to the shelf, the other items are not attached.

39. **Duck for cover** (page 26) The umbrellas top right and bottom left have the same design.

40. **From red to green!** (page 27)

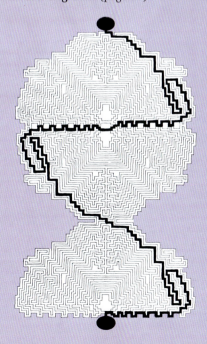

41. **Cheese chase** (pages 28 & 29) Only gate number 3 will get the mice to the cheese.

Tailend

Choose one of the snake's tails from the top. Follow its body to its head, and from that hexagon choose another snake's tail. Follow this tail to the snake's head, and continue this process until you come out at the bottom. Only one route will bring you to THE END!

The End